INNER CHILD

Published in 2023 by Welbeck
An imprint of Welbeck Non-Fiction Limited
part of Welbeck Publishing Group
Offices in: London – 20 Mortimer Street, London W1T 3JW &
Sydney – Level 17, 207 Kent St, Sydney NSW 2000 Australia
www.welbeckpublishing.com

Text © Welbeck 2023
Design and layout © Welbeck Non-fiction Limited 2023

ISBN 978-1-80279-599-8

Printed in China

10 9 8 7 6 5 4 3 2 1

INNER CHILD

10 WAYS TO REPARENT AND HEAL YOURSELF

TIFFANY TRIEU

WELBECK

"All grown-ups were once children,

but only few of them remember it."

-Antoine De Saint-Exupéry

"Tất cả người lớn đều từng là trẻ em,
nhưng chỉ một số ít người trong số họ
nhớ được điều đó."
-Antoine De Saint-Exupéry

CONTENTS

THIS BOOK
IS FOR YOU

1

My story starts with my parents. They came to the States in the 1970s as refugees of the American war in Vietnam, each taking their own journey across the ocean and crossing paths in Portland, Oregon. It was here where they found themselves in a completely new country, far away from any emotional and financial support they once had.

My mom and dad never talked about their past much, and since I had never been to the motherland myself, Vietnam felt like a made-up place. The only clues I had of where they were from were a few black-and-white photos, stories of how my dad dreamed of having a fridge filled to the brim with food when he arrived in the States, and, of course, the survival and fear that crept into their decisions daily. Together, they worked their way up. Not for the sake of climbing a corporate ladder, but to build a home. A home where there was enough food to eat and enough money to cover our basic needs.

Growing up, I not only felt the generational gap between me and my parents, but also the gap of being raised in different countries, different worlds. The values my parents held – collectivism, familial duty and honour – became a great source of conflict between us. These differences were exacerbated by the fact that they had spent most of their young adulthood living on Vietnamese land that had become the target of political turmoil, bombings and war. Surviving was their biggest concern. They didn't have

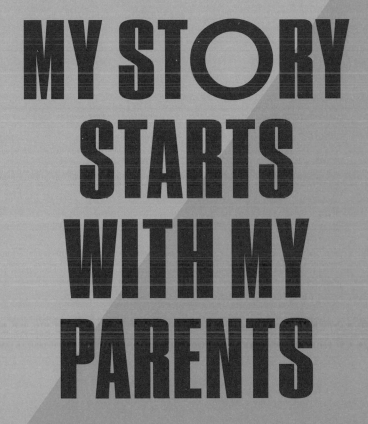

MY STORY STARTS WITH MY PARENTS

I WANTED A HOME THAT WAS BEYOND FOOD, SHELTER AND WARMTH

time and space for feelings during their escape over here, let alone dreams. I know many of you reading this, especially children of diaspora, may understand.

Being a child of refugees, a large part of my life has been reconciling the vast difference in reality between my parents' life in America and my life in America. As a child, I noticed all the ways my parents pushed aside their true feelings. I felt it in their relationship with money, with family and even with America.

I noticed when my dad chose to spend the weekend working extra hours, while my mom held in her sadness.

When they told us, "Friendships don't matter. Family is everything," mourning the life they had said goodbye to.

When they said, "Mỹ là number one. America is the best," counting the years since they had last visited Vietnam.

Their sacrifice was letting go of their own home to create a home for their children, but for me, I wanted a home that was beyond food, shelter and warmth. I wanted to be seen on the inside, not just for my outside accomplishments. I wanted to be valued for my sensitivity and awareness, not just my hard work and obedience. I wanted to know that there was room to fail and be loved at the same time. I wanted them to encourage me to hang out with friends and ask me how my day was. I wanted to communicate with them without language barriers, without telling me to stop crying, and without taking away my problems.

I blamed my parents for the pain I felt. I wished they were more American, that they were different people. I still have a voice inside who believes that, but blaming them only created more hurt, resentment and pain for me. They did the best they could. I was ready to grow and be my own person.

I WAS READY TO GROW

AND BE MY OWN PERSON

Empathizing with my parents doesn't mean the pain and hurt I experienced as a child isn't real. In fact, their struggle and my struggle can coexist. Yet, before I discovered who my inner child was, or more accurately, discovered the phrase "inner child" existed, it felt difficult to honour both my feelings and theirs. How could I feel angry, sad or disappointed if my parents denied those feelings themselves? Growing up in a household where my parents didn't have the capacity to hold me emotionally, I often bypassed my own feelings to hold theirs or accommodate for the reactions I thought they would have.

Healing my inner child has involved dedicating time and energy to feel my feelings, which is way harder than it sounds. Taking care of my needs as they come up. Being there for myself first, even if it means taking a moment for myself before being there for others. Healing my inner child means taking a break when I need to, instead of working harder to the brink of burnout. Healing my inner child looks like listening to my intuition and doing things in the way I want, even if it seems unconventional. Taking care of my inner child means communicating my boundaries to my family over and over again, even when they ask me, "Why?!" Taking care of myself and my inner child also means doing the hard things, such as asking friends for support, paying taxes and doing things we might not want to do.

All of us are here on our own journeys to discover our true selves. Part of that means untangling ourselves from the web of expectations woven by our parents, caretakers and even society. This journey is about coming home to ourselves. It is important to acknowledge there are many ways to do so.

In this book, we will focus on coming home by getting to know our inner children.

As you focus on nurturing a loving relationship with your inner self, you also transform how you relate to your friends, colleagues and possibly parents, whether they are present or not in your life. Connecting with your inner child, you will begin to notice a new-found confidence arise, one that has always been there. I am so excited for you to find your inner magic. Lean into yourself and listen. Perhaps you will find the *home* that has always been there.

In this book, I will share what I have learned through my research project called life, as well as through the dependable resources and people I have found along the way. Though this book is categorized under self-help, I would like to emphasize how important finding support and community is throughout your healing process, and this will feel challenging at times. You will notice I mention many people throughout the book who have guided me – because truly, it takes a village to raise a child.

Excited for you,

tiffany (thanh nguyệt)

THIS BOOK IS FOR YOU

...if you are curious to discover how it feels to create a safe, supportive environment within yourself.

The intention of healing your inner child isn't to have good days every day. It is so that your inner child knows your adult self is there for them and loves them, especially on the hard days.

Throughout this book, I will refer to your inner world and outer world. Your outer world is the world you see when you wake up, where you go about your daily lives – brushing your teeth, talking to friends, eating lunch, perhaps saying "hi" to neighbours. At the same time, you have a rich inner world, where your memories, dreams, hopes, desires – your conscious and subconscious – lie. This is where your inner child lives.

Our inner and outer lives are inextricably linked together. What we eat affects our mood, just as how we feel affects how we show up in life. Yet we are taught to spend most of our day focused on nurturing our outer life. When we exist in a society run by capitalism, focusing on productivity and outcomes, we lose our connection to our intuition and natural rhythms. Often the problems we seek to change in our outer life are connected to our inner life. When our inner and outer life aren't harmonious, because of reasons inside and outside of our control, we experience inner conflict that can contribute to depression, anxiety and other ailments. To take care of the inner is to take care of the outer.

Through knowing your inner world and inner child, you will also naturally:

- develop self-trust, also known as your intuition or inner knowing

- become aware of and shift the energy of your inner conversations, also known as self-talk

Whether you experienced a single traumatic incident or recurring conditions of abuse, neglect or instability growing up, your inner child is worthy of feeling safe and loved. We have all experienced childhood wounds to an extent. Childhood trauma can look like needing to be a source of emotional support for the adults in your life, constantly moving locations or being bullied. Childhood trauma can also happen on a more subtle, larger societal scale, such as not seeing yourself represented as a child in the world around you.

No matter your outer upbringing, as an adult you are now able to listen and tend to your inner child in ways they didn't receive before. Part of becoming an adult is knowing that you have the power to recognize your needs, ask for what you need and can resource yourself.

INNER CHILD, WHO ARE YOU?

Take a deep breath in through your nose, filling up your belly, and exhale from your mouth. Imagine a version of your younger self. Gently focus on their energy. Sense what they are wearing, how they look and any details that catch your attention.

Looking at this younger you, imagine if you told them they didn't matter. How would that feel? Could you do it? None of us want to be critical of ourselves, let alone our younger self; however, we do it more often than is easy to admit.

Before you move on, pause to thank your younger self for showing up, and let them know they do matter to you. Very much so.

Your inner child is a voice inside you, the part that stays with you even as you grow older. There are many versions of them, at different ages and timelines of your life. When talking about *inner child work* or *self-parenting*, we often pay attention to the *wounded inner child*, but I want you to take a moment to appreciate who your inner child naturally is.

They are the younger part of you. The baby straight out of the womb, crying as you take your first sip of fresh air, screaming in a room full of strangers, not giving a damn about all the noise you are making. Your inner child is the part of you who loves running in the field of grass, hands ripping up daisies, feeling as free as a bird. Your inner child is the you who stares

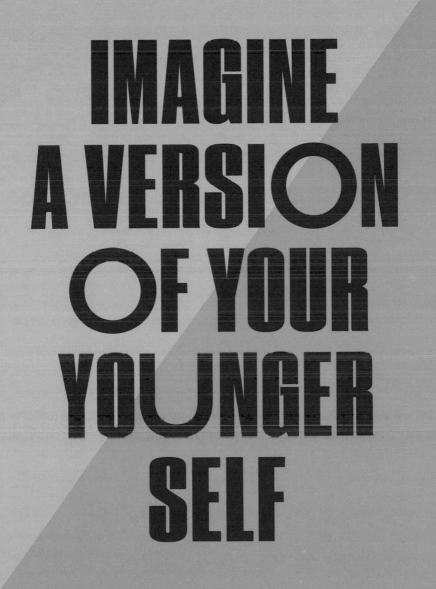

at fireworks in awe, mouth gaping, as though you are seeing magic for the first time.

Inner children are naturally curious. They may be loud, rambunctious and rebellious. They may be scared, shy and quiet. They are most likely a mix of all the above. Like children, they can be driven to please the adults in their life – such as your inner parent, which we will delve into in the self-parenting section – so that they can get the love and attention they crave. They are the YOU who will flourish with the right nurturing and care.

INNER CHILDREN ARE

NATURALLY CURIOUS

Your inner child holds an infinite range of expression, creativity and jubilance for life. No matter what happens in life, no one can take your inner child away.

Through all the traumas, big and small, the one thing that's for sure is the relationship you can create with your inner child. As you get to know them, like getting to know a friend, you will learn about their likes and dislikes – what makes them excited and what makes them feel vulnerable. Your inner children can be many different ages with different personalities. A version of your inner child who is shy may grow into a version who is bold and outspoken.

Another version of your inner child who had to be overly responsible and practical to survive may inspire you to play and dream bigger. The best part is, with your guidance, your inner child will grow and change with you. Together, you can let go of defence mechanisms and relational patterns that no longer serve the present you in adulthood.

Your inner child is the key to your aliveness, and as you nurture a safe, loving relationship with them, you can begin to soothe and address their wounds to make space for the following changes in your life.

CREATIVITY, PLAY AND SILLINESS

Unbound by society's standards and expectations, your inner child doesn't see rules; instead, they see more room for creative possibilities. Nothing feels too impractical or silly. Taking risks through creativity and play is possible, as your inner child knows they are unapologetically loved.

A SENSE OF SAFETY AND SECURITY WITHIN YOURSELF

When you're not disproportionally searching for external validation or reacting to your past wounds, you are more free to be present and secure in your outer relationships.

A DEEPER CONNECTION TO YOUR BODY

Children are tactile and in tune with their bodies. They allow their feelings to manifest and be expressed fully, even when it's not the most convenient timing. Uninhibited by social constructs, they don't place judgements on how their body looks or how they experience emotions. They only begin to pick up judgements about themselves by observing how the world around them responds.

SELF-TRUST AND INNER KNOWING

Children are intuitive. Before they learn the concept of "asking for permission", they trust themselves with what they want. Children don't ask for permission to feel, to express, to explore and to follow their intuition. They trust who they are, until they are told otherwise. Connecting to them is also connecting to your unabashed inner knowing.

YOUR LIFE ENERGY (QI) AND ALIVENESS

When your inner child is suppressed and silenced, they become lifeless and dull. The energy we use to squash our inner child can be channelled into uplifting them, and in turn, uplifting ourselves. Our inner child's aliveness leads us to be open to life's potentialities.

REFLECTION

Name a moment when you felt like a child this week. It can be a moment you feel good about or one you wish to grow from.

How did you feel at that moment? Did you notice any impulses, sensations or feelings arise in your body?

If you were to pause, what do you think your inner child wanted to tell you at that moment?

You can ask this question out loud, "Dear Inner Child, what were you trying to tell me when _____ happened?"

End the reflection by thanking your inner child for communicating with you. You can say, "Inner child, thank you for communicating with me."

As you live in a world where you are pushed to your limits to do more and be more, your inner child can help you come back to slowing down, feeling deeply and honouring what you need. Talking to your inner child may feel forced or awkward at first, but with time, you will get a fuller picture of who they are – and ultimately, of who you are through them.

NAME A
MOMENT
WHEN YOU
FELT LIKE
A CHILD
THIS WEEK

COMMITTING TO YOURSELF

3

As you get to know your inner child, think of your relationship with them in the same way you think of relationships with anyone else in your outer life. It will take some time for you to warm up to each other. You will slowly discover each other's quirks – where you are stubborn, where you are quite strange and where you both connect or butt heads.

Before you begin this journey to get to know your inner child, I invite you to do a few things.

- Get yourself a fresh journal, dedicated solely to this process. A large sketchbook is great to give you the flexibility to draw as well as write. This paper space will be your home base and will hold all the things you learn about your inner child.

- Choose a photo of your younger self, one that you will keep close by. Place it next to your mirror or somewhere you will see every day. This photo, of course, can be swapped out over time, whenever you feel like it. A physical photo is best, but if not, a digital one works, too.

- Take a moment to write why you are curious in getting to know your inner child. This will be a reminder for when the days get rough. When beginning to speak to your inner child, it is helpful to start your sentences with "Dear Inner Child" or "Inner Child".

IT WILL TAKE SOME TIME FOR YOU TO WARM UP TO EACH OTHER

INNER CHILD, I AM CURIOUS TO LEARN ABOUT YOU BECAUSE...

REFLECTION

Inner Child, I am curious to learn about you because

....
....
....
....
....
....
....
....
....
....
....
....
....
....
....
....
....
....
....
....
....
....

SELF-PARENTING

It was 2018. I had graduated from college two years before and got an internship at an exhibit design firm that turned into a full-time job. It seemed like the perfect opportunity. I was working in the field I studied in and I had enough money to pay off student loans.

But once the novelty of working wore off, I was exhausted. I was exhausted from commuting 1.5 hours each way, trying to fit into the idea of what it meant to be an adult, which seemed boring, drab and dry. I had donated all my colourful clothes, big roomy sweaters and "non-office wear" months before. No one had explicitly told me to do this, but a voice inside me was punishing me and didn't care if I was selling my soul away.

At some point I got tired of pretending but felt too shy to fully express myself. I believe humans are creative and resilient. We always find a way back to ourselves. So I did what I always loved to do. I made things. I crafted. I made myself some banana earrings out of shrinky dinks. To me, shrinky dinks reminded me of childhood.

I wore the earrings with pride each day while formulating my escape plan. I would work until I paid off my student loans. I did the maths and set the dates on my calendar. It would take me another six months working at this job. When the time came for me to put in my two weeks, it was obvious my manager agreed with my decision. She apologized for not giving me enough mentorship and I told her I understood. She had a lot on her plate, too.

I had left my job with the intention of allowing myself to do three things. I gave myself permission to:

1   make things with my hands

2   learn for myself (outside of being an employee)

3   find my own creative voice (outside the creativity that was pre-approved by my teacher, peers and workplace)

I was fortunate enough to live with my family while I figured things out. I knew it would be tough, but in no way did I expect how I felt during the following months. A month into sitting at home by myself, I was depressed. After I left my job, the structure I had been given by others in my life completely fell apart. With no school or work to tell me what to do, I had to decide for myself. I couldn't get up in the morning and would sleep in, not because it felt good, but because I had no good reason to wake up. I felt like no one would notice if I disappeared from the face of the Earth.

TALKING TO MY INNER CHILD EACH MORNING HELPED BRING JOY AND EXCITEMENT INTO MY DAY

One morning I remembered feeling so empty while I was sitting unshowered with the sun searing in my face at 11 a.m. I didn't want to feel this way anymore. I remembered a book I had read months ago. An accidental gift from my partner. An iconic yellow book called *Self-Parenting: The Complete Guide to Your Inner Conversations*. At that point, I remembered breezing through chapters of the book, feeling so validated that we all have inner voices that need to be heard. Our indecisiveness isn't a character flaw, instead, it is a sign for us to listen deeply to the voices inside and resolve the conflict between them. Through his self-parenting technique, Dr John K Pollard III specifically teaches us how to connect with both our inner child and inner parent.

At that point, I was willing to try anything to help myself feel better. So I sat down every morning to talk to my inner child, following the book's prompts. Morning sessions became a reason for me to wake up. Talking to my inner child each morning helped bring joy and excitement into my day. My inner parent – which we will delve into later – worked with my inner child to get things done and make sure her needs were taken care of, too.

After reading this book, I realized that I had been listening to my inner child all along, parenting her through my post-college situation. The moment my inner child felt stifled by my lack of self-expression became a chance for me to change how I perceived what "being an adult" looked like. When I decided to leave my job was when my inner parent freed my inner child from conforming to a system that didn't work for her.

As I came into a conscious relationship with my inner child, I was able to move through daily to-dos and responsibilities while respecting the younger part of me who wanted to play, dance, sing and have fun with friends. I learned I didn't need to put my inner child away to be an adult.

Since then, I have had the chance to learn about the inner child from many more books and people. So many tools have helped me, such as Internal Family Systems (an integrative model of psychotherapy), breathwork (conscious controlled breathing) and somatics (understanding the language of your body).

As you read this book, I invite you to revisit why you want to reconnect with your inner child.

I LEARNED
I DIDN'T NEED TO
PUT MY INNER CHILD
AWAY TO BE
AN ADULT

REFLECTION

When have you trusted your inner child?

....
....
....
....
....

Describe how your inner child helped you in that situation or in making that decision.

....
....
....
....
....

How do you feel in discovering or rediscovering that you have trusted your inner child before?

....
....
....
....
....

Now that you have the opportunity, how would you like to thank them?

....
....
....
....
....

Again, you may begin by saying, "Inner Child, thank you for _____"

Self-parenting is the process of consciously reconnecting to your inner child, providing them with the love and care they needed, but didn't necessarily receive. Parenting your inner child can help them heal from past traumas, redefine past coping mechanisms and mature healthily. You may also hear the term "re-parenting". We will use these two words interchangeably here.

WHAT IS CONSCIOUS

SELF-PARENTING?

I specify "conscious self-parenting" here because whether you have been conscious or not, you have been parenting your inner child all this time. However, the voice who currently parents your inner child, also known as your inner parent, may not be the voice who is most supportive to your growth now.

To talk about self-parenting, it is helpful to define who your inner parent is.

WHO IS MY INNER PARENT?

Your inner parent is the voice inside you, made up of the caretakers, teachers, guides and authority figures in your life. When beginning to self-parent, your inner parent may initially sound like what you may call your "inner critic". This is because the adults who took care of you had their own insecurities and judgements, which were then passed down to you. Children accept these inner voices as truths, not knowing that adults, too, have unresolved wounds.

When you choose to consciously parent your inner child, you have the potential to break the pattern of wounds passed down from generation to generation, also known as "intergenerational trauma". Parenting not only happens on a caregiver to child level, but also in how you are taught by the education system and treated by your environment.

Dr John K Pollard III categorizes the inner parent into the "negative inner parent" and "positive inner parent". Your negative inner parent criticizes, belittles and judges. They use power tactics to manipulate and control your inner child. This voice may feel so blended into your personality or way of navigating the world that you may wonder, "If I don't scare myself or force myself into doing _____, then I won't have the self-discipline to do it!"

This is where your positive inner parent comes in. With the right amount of support, discipline and attunement to your inner child, your positive inner parent guides your inner child to develop a strong sense of self by respecting their thoughts and feelings. Your positive inner parent also sets boundaries and makes sure you are completing the tasks and responsibilities you need to do, while considering your inner child's capacity. Your positive inner parent provides your inner child with a strong sense of security. They are the home your inner child can come back to, in good times and bad.

Re-parenting your inner child doesn't erase the harm you may have experienced in your actual childhood, but everyone deserves to give their inner child a second chance at receiving the love and care they should have received. As you re-parent your inner child, you can help them to let go of defence mechanisms that no longer work for you and remain open to new possibilities. In doing so, you will see a real transformation in your everyday life as an adult and your ability to connect with others.

WHAT KIND OF RELATIONSHIP WOULD YOU LIKE TO NURTURE WITH YOUR INNER CHILD?

REFLECTION

What kind of relationship would you like to nurture with your inner child?

....

....

....

....

Everyone's ideal relationship with their inner child is unique to them. Your answer will likely expand over time.

Dear Inner Child, what would you like people to know about you?

....

....

....

....

Take a moment to begin listening to your inner child.

Take a deep breath before answering this prompt, close your eyes and place a hand on your heart.

Ask this prompt out loud.

A close friend of mine wrote a short letter:

"Dear Inner Child,

I'm sorry. For ignoring you all these years.

I'm sorry you didn't get to let people know who you truly are.

Instead, we showed ourselves down to tiny, micro-sized bits and pieces of ourselves, of you.

And you didn't deserve that.

You want people to know that you deserve love. Love, as innocent summer days playing in the park sands were swapped with trips to the hospital. Sleepovers spent at your Auntie Letty's now exchanged for overnight, bedside hand-holding.

You want people to know that you were once happy and that you can still find that happiness. Joy, even as laughter turned to yells and sadness evolved to everlasting sorrow. You want people to know that you can still laugh and smile.

Finally, you want everyone to know that you're still a child. Even after spelling books were traded for billing statements and slurpees were discarded for liquid thickeners.

You want people to know that you're still here.
I see that now.

Will you let me back in?

Love, Mac"

A poem from my Inner Child.

"I would like people to know I am just like
them.

I am strong.

I am weak.

I am curious.

I am scared.

I am brave. I can do anything!

But I want you to hold my hand.

I want you to comfort me.

And I just want people to know,

I am here!"

CREATING RITUALS OF SAFETY

You may have noticed that we begin every reflection and activity by welcoming in our inner child.

Creating rituals with my inner child has been essential in my healing. Rituals can be any set of actions performed with intention and care, paired with a beginning and an end. Rituals create an environment of safety and predictability that is foundational during the first few years of childhood, helping the child develop secure attachment. With secure attachment, children know that even when their caretakers leave, they will come back for them.

Just as we can transform an everyday activity, such as making coffee, into a ritual, we can create rituals around connecting to our inner child. By actively inviting your inner child in, you signal to them: "You now have my full attention." Your opening ritual can look like putting your phone on silent, playing a calming song or taking a deep breath together.

Once your time together is ending, you can consciously thank your inner child for spending time with you. Your closing ritual can be a hug, an endearing phrase or a simple thank you. Even if you only have a few minutes, it is important for you to close out your time together. In this way, you show your inner child that you respect them and are thankful for their time.

SHOW YOUR INNER CHILD THAT YOU ARE THANKFUL FOR THEIR TIME

Another facet you can add to your ritual is finding a nickname both you and your inner child like. For many of the examples included, I have used "Inner Child" for simplicity and consistency.

CREATE A RITUAL WITH YOUR INNER CHILD

ACTIVITY

Create a ritual with your inner child. Use this to invite
your inner child in before journaling, visualizing or
playing.

Inner Child, how would you like to be referred to?
You can use a nickname or nicknames.

How would you like to say "hi" and "bye" together?

Continue to practice this ritual every time you meet,
until your inner child becomes as familiar with you as
your inner parent. Over time, you won't need to be so
formal, as they have developed trust in you. Your ritual
of "hello" and "goodbye" can be as casual as a quick
run-in with a friend.

In the next few sections, I will talk about all the ways
you can bond with your inner child, from visualizations
and journaling to playtime. And of course, you can
create your own activities together, too.

CONVERSATIONAL JOURNALING

When I was in elementary school, I kept a pink diary with orange fluff on the sides. It was my favourite confidant. I wrote in it almost every day, scribbling my deepest darkest thoughts, confessing my feelings for my crushes and documenting the details of each day. As I got older and life got busy, I forgot about the magic of journaling.

Beginning to journal again, I noticed three different styles of journaling: free-style, structure through prompts and something in between. The conversational journaling technique by Dr John K Pollard III provided me with enough structure to guide me while giving me enough room for flexibility. This technique gives you the lively back-and-forth rhythm of a text message conversation, alongside the tangible sincerity of a handwritten letter.

I've noticed this style of journaling is particularly useful for working through inner conflict, anywhere from the daily "What should I do today?" to navigating and soothing big emotions. After speaking to my inner child daily for at least a month, I begin to hear her voice more clearly inside me. By separating my inner parts, I allow each part to exist fully as they are, making it easier to observe and understand them.

Journaling allows you to spend quality time with your inner child and get to know them as you would any other person. Once you get to know them better and the trust between you grows, you will be able to work through inner conflicts with each other. Journaling allows you to intentionally enter the inner conversations you already have, by providing a space to slow down and to learn how you speak to your inner child. Plus, all you need is a journal and to set aside some time.

For the first session with your inner child, you as the inner parent will write a letter to:

- introduce yourself

- let your inner child know your intention(s) with these journaling sessions

- make any amends that need to happen

In this initial session, you will simply pay attention to how your inner child receives your message. Then in the following days, get to know your inner child by asking them simple questions.

Inner Parent (IP):

Hi, Inner Child, it's me, tiffany.

I know it's been a very long time since we spoke.
I'm sorry it's taken so long for us to sit down
together. Over 20 years, in fact! I would like to get
to know you better if you would let me. I want to
understand what makes you happy or sad. What you
like and don't like. I would like to be there for it all.
And if you can be patient with me, I would like to be
a better Inner Parent to you.

HOW AN INITIAL

SESSION COULD LOOK

In fact, I'd love to meet every day for the next month after we wake up and brush our teeth. How does that sound? Please let me know whatever it is you need.

The one who wants to know you best.

Your Inner Parent,

tiffany

FORMATTING YOUR JOURNAL

For the sessions after this, we will format the page in two columns. You can fold your paper vertically, hot-dog style, when starting out. Technically, you don't need to physically fold your paper in half for this to work, but it's a soothing ritual to begin your conversational journaling practice. There will also be some space in this book for you to give it a go.

Once you fold the paper in half, you have two columns. Think of each column as a space for each inner voice to talk. For the first few sessions, it's helpful to dedicate the left side (the column you read first) to your inner parent and the right side (the column you read second) to your inner child. Another way to think about this is whoever is leading the conversation will be in the column you read first. The person taking the lead is like a facilitator of inner conversation, usually initiating communication, asking questions and guiding where the conversation goes.

The inner parent and inner child voices aren't forever tied to their respective left and right sides, but in the beginning of these journaling sessions, it's helpful for the inner parent to take the lead in repairing the relationship as they have the tools to do this. After multiple sessions, you may notice a natural shift where your inner child feels comfortable enough to initiate conversations. This is a great sign and shows they are feeling more like themself around you. Remember to celebrate this moment along the way!

THE PERSON TAKING THE LEAD IS LIKE A FACILITATOR OF INNER CONVERSATION

IT'S NORMAL THAT YOUR INNER CHILD FEELS HESITANT ABOUT THIS PROCESS

HOW A SECOND SESSION WITH YOUR INNER CHILD MAY LOOK

It's normal that your inner child feels hesitant about this process. If so, you can spend the first few sessions imagining that you, as the inner parent, are sitting beside them. This will allow them to be completely themselves rather than forcing closeness.

Inner Parent (IP):

Hello, Inner Child. It's me again, your Inner Parent. How are you doing today?

Inner Child (IC):

I am okay. How are you?

IP: Oh, thank you for asking me.

I'm doing very well. I've been excited to talk to you.

How do you feel about us having these sessions?

IC: It's weird. I don't really trust you.

IP: That makes a lot of sense.

We have just met! How about we just sit together?

IC: Okay, I would like that!

Imagine sitting with your inner child for however long you would like to. Then end your session with a thank you or a closing ritual. For me it looks like saying thank you to myself and my inner child for showing up.

IP: Thank you for your time with me today, Inner Child.

I'll come visit you again tomorrow after we brush our teeth!

IC: Okay.

CHOOSING APPROPRIATE TOPICS

Choose some topics to ask your inner child as they begin to feel more comfortable.

These are ordered from easy questions to more advanced ones, as the conversations with your inner child will gradually feel more engaging as the relationship progresses:

Check-ins

- How are you feeling today?

- Would you like to tell me more about that?

"Favourites" and "Not Favourites"

- What is your favourite food or snack?

- What is your favourite memory?

- What is your favourite animal?

- What do you like to do for fun?

- Who are your favourite people?

- What are your pet peeves?

- What bores you?

Activities to do together

- What do you want to do together?

- How would you like to celebrate your birthday?

- What makes you feel really loved?

Making decisions together

- Share your daily agenda with your inner child and collaborate with your inner child to create rewards that benefit you both.

- Make space for your inner child and inner parent to voice their perspective before coming to a consensus.

GUIDELINES FOR SELF-PARENTING

- **Intention is powerful.** Dr John K Pollard III recommends dedicating 45 minutes a day to this practice; however, even dedicating ten minutes a day to journaling with your inner child is a solid place to start. I promise, you'll be so enamoured by your inner child, it will be easy to continue meeting with them and to extend your time together gradually.

- **Ask questions aloud as you are writing them.** Speaking aloud helps differentiate your inner child from your inner parent voice, especially when you are beginning this practice.

- **Loving boundaries with your inner child is possible.** Your job as an inner parent isn't to appease your inner child's every need and want. Instead you, as an inner parent, are here to acknowledge and validate their thoughts and feelings. It's about creating a safe space where your inner child is heard and you can include them in decisions and creating boundaries that are beneficial for you both.

- **Centre your inner child's experience.** When your inner child is expressing a feeling that makes you uncomfortable, don't defend or justify your action or inaction. Instead, listen and affirm them.

- **Meet your inner child where they are.** The way your inner child and inner parent speak to one another depends on the age of the inner child you are speaking to. For example, when you are speaking to your inner baby, you may want to address them as baby. Your inner baby may address you as mum, mummy, dad or daddy. It is healthy to allow your inner child to communicate in a way that comes naturally to them. By allowing them to be at the age or maturity level they are at, you as the inner parent are respecting your inner child's own pace. You may find the younger versions of your inner child needing more attention and care, and that is completely normal.

- **Pay attention to the full range of your inner child's expressions**. Note how they respond to how you communicate to them, through their body language, how they sound, etc. In this way, you can learn how your inner child prefers to be tended to. Notice when they are feeling distant and removed or feeling like they need to fight to be heard. Either can happen when they expect their needs not to be met.

- **Be patient with your inner child.** Like any relationship, building trust with your inner child will take time. Accept that getting to the place you want to be with your inner child may take longer than you had hoped and that that's okay.

As an adult, you are given a second chance in meeting your inner child's unfulfilled needs through your inner parent's love and care.

Your journaling sessions may look different from mine, and again, that is a good sign. It means you are listening to what is true to you. If you don't resonate with writing down your inner conversations, you can use the same technique to speak to your inner child out loud. You can use a portable recorder to do daily audio journaling rather than write. If you're feeling playful, you can channel your inner parent and inner child with some voice acting. This is fun to do in the shower before you begin your day or while you are winding down from it.

Lastly, think of a journaling session with your inner child as a date. Invite yourself to make it feel special. Take yourself to a nearby park or sit in your favourite spot as you have your session. Before you know it, you will be able to carry the feeling of home and safety that you've created during these sessions with you wherever you go.

AS AN ADULT, YOU ARE GIVEN A SECOND CHANCE IN MEETING YOUR INNER CHILD'S UNFULFILLED NEEDS

VISUALIZATIONS

YOU CAN CREATE
A SPACE BETWEEN
YOUR DREAM
WORLD AND YOUR
WAKING WORLD

VISUALIZATIONS

A visualization is a meditation focused on dreaming. Through visualizations, you can create a space between your dream world and your waking world. Visualizations provide you with the space to imagine, process and heal in ways you may not be able to do in reality. In this space, you get to activate all your senses, which integrates your entire brain, categorized in three parts as coined by Dr Daniel Siegel: the reptilian brain, mammalian brain and human brain.

- The reptilian brain, your brain stem, is responsible for your sense of physical safety and security.

- The mammalian brain, your limbic system, is responsible for your associations with attachment, love and belonging.

- The human brain, your cortex, is responsible for integration between your inner and outer world, processing and taking in new information.

Visualizations activate all three parts of your brain, making them powerful in creating new associations and reprogramming your body and mind.

The first time I was guided through a visualization, I remember wondering if it was okay to dream this big. In this in-between state, I peeled back the layers of armour I had built up over the years and found a version of me who was imaginative and expansive. She also carried a type of wisdom I hadn't dared tap into since I was a kid – the ability to trust.

In the years following this, I guided myself through visualizations before big presentations or whenever I needed to restore faith in where I was going. It wasn't until I worked with my past therapist, who

TRY A SHORT,

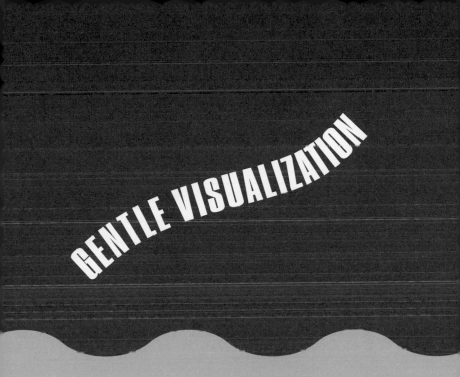

GENTLE VISUALIZATION

gave me the information I needed, that I understood why visualizations are so powerful in helping us feel grounded and connected to ourselves.

Before you get into your head too deep with the nitty gritty details, try a short, gentle visualization. One that leans more into what you are feeling instead of what you are seeing.

VISUALIZATION: *RU NGỦ*, A LULLABY

Ru Ngủ means "rocking to sleep" or a "lullaby" in Vietnamese. This visualization will focus on the feeling of soothing your inner child by holding yourself, a practice you can go back to time and time again.

To set up this visualization, find a space in which you feel comfortable enough to close your eyes and hum. Pick a calming song you would like to hum to, with or without lyrics. Choose a song you already know and are comforted by; one of my favourite songs to listen to while holding my inner child is "O, I Love You" by Essie Jain.

Get cosy. Taking a seat or laying down. If the weather is more chilly, add a blanket to cosy up in. If you have a ritual to invite in your inner child, do this now.

Invite yourself to take a few deep breaths. Soften your gaze. Throughout the visualization, imagine soothing your inner child physically. You can use the butterfly hug to ground you. The butterfly hug is when you cross your hands over your chest, connecting at the thumbs. As you take deep breaths, you can pat your chest, alternating sides. You can adjust this technique to however you'd like. I like to imagine it more as hugging myself, crossing my arms so that I can pat my forearms, and then patting right, left, right, left. The butterfly hug can be used outside of this visualization to ground yourself when you feel overwhelmed.

Continue self-soothing while sitting with your inner child and humming with them. You are holding them as you are holding yourself. Allow yourself to sway, move and sing. See if you can sense your younger self within you. Breathe with your feelings and sensations to let them pass. Continue until you feel complete with the practice.

Thank yourself and your inner child for participating.

Congratulations, you have done your first visualization with your inner child. Revisit this visualization with different songs and slowly you will have a playlist made just for your inner child!

VISUALIZE SITUATIONS OF SAFETY AND EASE

CREATING POSITIVE VISUALIZATIONS

During a visualization guided by my past therapist, I had imagined my mom running down a grassy hill with me. Here she was, completely present and attuned to my emotional needs. I held her hand as we ran in the lush green field, rolling into the grass and staring at the big open sky. The clouds looked perfect, fluffy and gorgeous. I was giggling, laughing, filled with pure bliss. Through the visualization, I experienced a level of emotional trust between us that was greater than I had ever felt before.

As my therapist and I ended the visualization, a pang of concern arose in me. "Am I just tricking myself for visualizing such a scene?"

My therapist smiled and reassured me that our reptilian brain, also known as our brain stem, is in charge of whether or not we go into flight or fight mode. By creating memories of emotional trust through the visualization, I strengthened the neural pathway that says, "Yes, it is safe to let your guard down. It is safe to be open to new possibilities."

Just as you can visualize all the ways a situation can go wrong, you can use the same ability to visualize situations of safety and ease. Your reptilian brain doesn't know the difference between what you see in your visualization and in your reality. In this way, positive visualizations can be used to reprogramme old defence mechanisms that keep you from trusting new people in your life or being open to a new way of relating in an existing relationship.

In addition to guiding yourself through visualizations, you can prime your body with your breath. Conscious controlled breathing is also known as breathwork. Your breath controls your body's physiological response (how your body feels), which then connects to how your brain's mental state, body and mind feed into each other.

During visualizations, you may like to begin them with deep belly breaths, as opposed to shallow chest breathing. This sends your body the message, "We have space to relax. We are safe." This breath is also called the Buddha Belly Breath.

To practice a Buddha Belly Breath, you inhale through the nose, sending air into your belly, expanding it like a balloon to match the golden Buddha statues with big bellies, then do a slow open-mouth exhale. This breath may feel unnatural when first practicing, as you normally breathe into your chest. You may want to hold off on deep belly breathing right after a full meal because this will feel very uncomfortable!

PRIME YOUR BODY WITH YOUR BREATH

VISUALIZATION: INNER CHILD, LET'S BE FRIENDS

This visualization is near and dear to my heart and one I developed in the very beginning of facilitating inner child workshops. It is best when guided by someone else, but if that isn't possible for you, feel free to record yourself reading this aloud.

The intention of this visualization is for you to viscerally meet your inner child. For a more advanced version of this visualization, you will bring your inner child to their favourite place.

As usual, find a comfortable seat and take a few deep belly breaths. Close your eyes or soften your gaze.

Take a moment to look around your existing space with your eyes closed. Take in the colours and objects that stand out to you and the sounds and smells. Recreating the room you are in within your mind helps warm up your imagination.

As you take a deep breath in and out, you hear a soft knock on your door. Today, you are expecting your inner child. Take a moment before you open the door to notice which feelings are coming up for you. Are you nervous, excited, scared?

When you open the door, you see a small figure emerge from behind it. Notice what they are doing. Are they wriggling about? Shy? Jumping off the walls?

This first moment with your inner child is precious. Introduce yourself and why you are here. Is there a way they would like you to greet them? A hug, a wave, a high-five?

At this point in the visualization, you can decide to stay in the room with your inner child and continue having a conversation, or, for a more advanced visualization, you can ask your inner child where they would like to go and play with you today.

In either situation, take the time to ask your inner child what they would like. Be patient with their replies. Notice their verbal and nonverbal cues. Praise them for communicating with you.

As you walk through the door together, you are transported to the place they want to go with you today. You can hold their hand and let them take you around, showing you all the things they want to do together. Note the things that stand out to you.

Once you feel ready, let your inner child know it is time to go. Make space for a proper goodbye. Once you do, give your inner child a hug, give yourself a hug. Slowly, let your inner child melt into you. Place your hands on your heart, where they will always stay with you.

Take a final deep breath to close out the visualization. Flutter your eyes open if they were closed.

LET YOUR INNER

CHILD MELT INTO YOU

For longer visualizations such as this one, you can keep a journal close by to jot down details that have come up. Use your notes to inspire future playdates with your inner child.

My best visualization experiences are when I am relaxed and cosy, sitting with a blanket or laying down. The more visualizations you practice, the more creative you'll be with setting up the mood and dreaming up ways to transition from one world to another.

VISUALIZATION: CASS'S BREATH

This visualization was kindly shared with me by Cassandra Lam, Somatic Healing Facilitator and Collective Rest Guide. Its intention is to remind us how interconnected our own breath is to our inner child's.

Settle in, either seated or laying down. Closing your eyes or softening your gaze, ask your inner child to take a seat facing you. Invite them to sit as close or as far to you as they feel comfortable to that day. Then place one hand on your chest, the other on your belly. This will help you stay connected to your body as you are breathing. Again, practice the Buddha Belly Breath, inhaling through your nose, filling up your belly, and exhale slowly with your mouth open.

As you breathe, imagine your breath connecting to your inner child's. Your inner child's exhale becomes your inhale. Your exhale will feed into your inner child's inhale. As you breathe, see if you can fill in the image of your inner child, the silhouette of their body, a smile, lines of their face. Note the detail without hanging onto it. Allow your breath to carry you through the visualization.

Explore ways you can invite your inner child deeper, such as inviting them to hold hands while breathing together. Continue until you feel complete.

Like all other practices, thank yourself and your inner child for participating.

Intense emotions can come up during visualizations, especially because they give you time to pause, sit with your feelings and engage with your full spectrum of senses. Tears are normal, so bring tissues and set aside a generous amount of time to be with yourself during and afterwards when possible. Most of all, know that you are the creator of your own experience, how far you go and where you take it. You can have full agency to pause at any time. Having that choice itself is powerful.

INTENSE EMOTIONS CAN COME UP DURING VISUALIZATIONS

PLAY AND CREATIVITY

ASK YOUR INNER CHILD HOW YOU CAN MAKE A BORING, EVERYDAY TASK FUN

If we were to simplify the process of healing our inner child – which is and will be messy and nonlinear – we can look at it in three parts: re-parenting our inner child, embodying our inner child and integrating the healing we've experienced internally into our outer relationships. Through play and creativity, we give ourselves the chance to embody our inner child.

As kids, we are slowly taught the many rules of how to act. "Stop fidgeting! Pay attention. Sit up straight. Don't play with your food." Do you remember what you were told?

For me, it was, "Study first! If you have too much fun now, you will suffer later." That last one really stuck with me. I didn't know what was "fun" versus "too much fun", so eventually my brain associated any fun with anticipated suffering.

When pleasure becomes linked with shame and guilt, play feels like a thing to be earned, rather than a joy we innately deserve. When we don't allow ourselves to play as adults, not only are we robbing ourselves of this pleasure, we are also sending a message to our inner child that there is no room for them in this world, when in fact it is our inner child's imagination and creativity that changes the world.

As an adult, ask your inner child how you can make a boring task fun. Set out 10 to 15 minutes to play. If, like me, you came from a family of workaholics, it will feel difficult to justify any playtime at all. Consult your inner child about it and see what they have to say. Over time, your window of exploration will grow and you'll get more comfortable having longer playtime. Your inner parent can trust that even when you play, things will be okay.

The great thing about play is that there is no right answer. There is no product expected from it at the end of the day. Play is for you to explore, express depths of yourself you don't normally get to. Shed a few layers of the person you need to be normally, and before you know it, your inner child will be the one helping you play.

YOU'LL GET MORE COMFORTABLE IN HAVING LONGER PLAYTIME

REFLECTION

Inner Child, what rules were we expected to follow?

Notice the feeling that comes up when writing each rule. Do you notice the intention behind them? You may still agree with an aspect of these rules or now notice the biases or fears they carry. Rules are given to children as a way of providing structure in a world they are still learning about, but these rules, too, are subjective, shaped by the people who created them.

Now you get a chance to update these old rules because you have outgrown them or they were too rigid to begin with. Rather than rules, give your inner child permission and guidelines that give them freedom and structure.

What permission or guidelines would you give yourself now? You can use the following phrases:

• I allow myself to

....

....

• I give myself permission to

....

....

For myself, I rewrite my rules.

Don't dye your hair. Don't wear revealing clothing.

I give myself space to express myself freely.

Don't stay up past midnight.

I give myself space to enjoy during the day, so I feel good when it's time for bed.

Don't sleep past eight in the morning.

I give myself space to sleep in when I want and need to.

Take the time to write down the conscious and unconscious rules you were held to. Rewriting them as your own adult will help your inner child to grow and mature with you.

....
....
....
....
....
....
....

WAYS YOU CAN PLAY WITH YOUR INNER CHILD

To play is truly a way of existing. It is how you navigate everyday tasks and situations, but sometimes all you need is a little scheduled recess. These activities are fun dates you can set up with your inner child, and of course, make your own!

GOING ABSTRACT

Abstract is a great way to release expectations and not get so hung up on the details. Choose your favourite medium or one you don't know at all. Colouring, drawing, collaging, painting ... It can be helpful to give yourself a guiding question, so you can go unhinged elsewhere. For example: How would you like to express your anger? What does sadness look like?

DRESS-UP TIME

Halloween isn't the only time for dress-up. You get to dress up as your favourite characters, play with some make-up, do your hair a little different. Which personalities and alter egos would you like to play into today?

A GIFT FROM THE BOTTOM OF MY HEART

Your inner child loves to connect and please others. One of the sweetest ways to do this is making a gift for someone you love. Think of someone you love, who you would like to express love to. Make a simple gift for them, nothing too fancy. Think fridge drawings, glitter glue, pompoms, picture frames made with dried pasta.

SOMETIMES THE BEST WAY TO GET TO KNOW YOUR INNER CHILD IS HEARTFELT QUALITY TIME

QUALITY TIME

Sometimes the best way to get to know your inner child is heartfelt quality time.

IT'S A DATE!

Take yourself and your inner child on an outing. Do all the things you've wanted to do. Get ice cream before dinner, go to that café you've been eyeing, buy that little knick-knack that makes your inner child happy. The more you suppress your inner child's wants and needs, the more vicious they'll come back to bite you later. The little things matter.

SINGALONG TIME

When you find yourself feeling emotions, big or small, sing them! Take yourself on a walk, give yourself a bath, cook yourself a yummy meal and sing your heart out. If someone happens to catch you in the middle of a song, flash them a smile because they'll most likely be enjoying your song, too.

MIRROR TALK

You're really nervous. Maybe you're going on a first date, giving a big presentation, meeting a friend for the first time. Take time to look at yourself and talk your feelings out with your inner child.

LOOK, MA, I GOT FRIENDS

Connect to your inner child with a friend! You both might just learn a new thing or two about each other.

LET'S TRADE

Remember when you used to trade your CapriSun for a Kool-Aid? Pokémon pencil toppers for a mini stapler? Or is that just me? There's something about the thrill of trading with your friend as a child. Sometimes you didn't get the best deal, but it was fun anyway. Well, you can still do this as an adult: think of a theme for your trade and when you want to do it. It can be as grandiose or as simple as you'd like.

SNAIL MAIL

Who doesn't love snail mail? Handwritten letters and having pen pals surpasses any kind of online messaging. Ask a friend to be your pen pal and deck out your letters with all the stickers, photos and goodies you have always wanted.

PLAYFUL MOVEMENT

Here are some fun movement activities you can do with your inner child, courtesy of my friend, somatic healer and facilitator of feeling free, Monica Climaco.

STILL GOT THE MOVES?

Pick a dance from your childhood: the sprinkler, the chicken dance, the disco move, electric slide. Then pick a song you're really into now. See if you can fit the same moves into the songs you're listening to now or throwback songs that make you cringe – just a little.

PASS IT ON!

Pull a friend onto the dance floor with you. Pass on your dance moves to them. Let them pass their dance moves onto you. You may learn a new thing or two.

RESISTANCE TO PLAY

While making time to play, you may feel resistance coming up. Rather than brushing these inner voices aside, listen to what they are saying and note where they may be coming from. Acknowledge and thank them. All they need is reassurance from you that they are heard and they are safe to take a step back.

When I am feeling anxious to get back to work or back to being "serious", even when I have scheduled a break, I define a window of exploration for myself. I tell my inner parent, "Let's see what happens when we play for five minutes." Slowly, my inner parent will realize it is both safe and symbiotic for my inner child to play. We will still fulfil our responsibilities and, more importantly, we will learn how to truly take care of ourselves.

Understand how much time, energy and rest you need to get things done rather than simply pushing through. In the long run, you will trust yourself more deeply to come back to the work you need to do and the responsibilities you need to take on because you haven't sacrificed your inner child to be an adult.

REFLECTION

When I am playing, I feel

....

....

....

....

....

....

....

When I allow myself to play, it brings _____
into my life.

MAKING TIME FOR CONNECTION

Whichever way you choose to connect with your inner child, I encourage you to intentionally meet with them every day for at least one month up to three months.

Like becoming friends with someone new, the quality time you spend with each other matters. Researcher Jeffrey Hall found that it takes 200 hours to develop a "best friendship" with another person. Of course, there are no hard and fast rules for becoming friends. You aren't trying to keep an hourly log here, but if Hall's study shows you one thing, it's that your inner child will certainly feel your intention and dedication.

As you feel more settled into your relationship with your inner child, you can explore what it means to consciously connect to your inner child alongside trusted company or in community. Being able to express how your inner child feels and what they want with people who are on a similar healing journey can be affirming and freeing to the soul. As my breathwork coach Andrea Maeng has told me, "Any feeling you have felt or thought you have thought, chances are someone else has, too."

YOU CAN BE CREATIVE WITH HOW YOU WANT TO SPEND INTENTIONAL QUALITY TIME WITH YOUR INNER CHILD

GOING DEEPER

7

My first visceral memory of anger was when I was ten. I was downstairs all by myself one night. I don't know what sparked it, but all I remember was jumping on the dining room table, squatting on the very corner of it. As I jumped down, I felt red-hot, hands beating at my chest. Pretending I was an ape, I huffed and puffed. I felt powerful and strong, all the rageful energy rushing upwards inside me. My body filled with the pure belief that nothing could stand in my way. Nothing could shake me.

I think of this memory whenever I'm afraid of feeling my anger now, remembering how whole and free I felt then. Connecting back to that feeling makes me wonder where I learned to fear anger in the first place. I either saw anger expressed in ways that resulted in destruction and harm – yelling matches, plates being thrown and shattered, and physical violence – or anger being suppressed into cold shoulders and passive aggressive stares. I thought if I felt anger and let it get past a certain point, I would hurt my parents and the people around me. I learned not to trust my anger. Ironically, the more fearful I was of my anger, the quicker I was to lash out when my feelings became too intense to bottle up. I thought the only options I had were to suppress, numb or redirect. Little did I know the ten-year-old me already knew the answer. Her anger was an opportunity to connect back to her body and true self.

I FELT POWERFUL AND STRONG. NOTHING COULD SHAKE ME

REFLECTION

What is your relationship with anger?

....
....
....
....
....
....
....

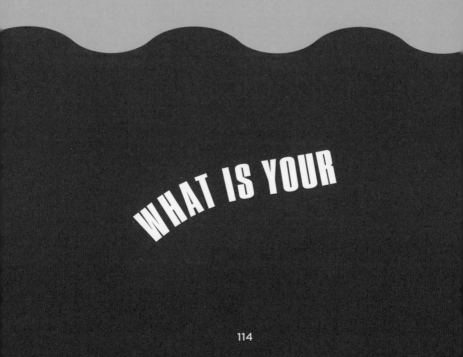

WHAT IS YOUR

RELATIONSHIP WITH ANGER?

Is there a memory you have with anger that you are proud of?

....

....

....

....

....

....

....

....

UNDERSTAND OUR EMOTIONS

Anger is here to help us set boundaries, stand up for injustices and listen to our gut. What we fear is not the emotion itself, but the expression of emotion. The harmful expressions we see, the outbursts, result from fear of feeling the emotion. When we fear feeling the emotion, we treat the emotion as if it were a hot potato. We throw it back at them, yelling, "Hey! You made me feel this way, and I don't like it! Take this!" We may also feel ashamed that this emotion is coming up at all, so we take our emotions and hide them in the closet, hoping no one will notice. Stuffing them deeper and deeper inside until the closet bursts.

Our emotions are here to guide us, not hurt us. As we learn to hold difficult emotions and allow the feelings to move through us, emotions become energy we can work with. *Emotion* is derived from the Latin word *emotere*, meaning energy in motion. In that sense, emotions are neither good nor bad. They are here to support us in transforming into who we want to be. Our body knows no difference from good or bad, only uncomfortable and comfortable. This is why when we numb ourselves from the "difficult" emotions such as anger, fear and sadness, we also end up numbing ourselves from the "good" emotions we want to feel. When we learn to feel an emotion from a place of

OUR EMOTIONS ARE HERE TO GUIDE US, NOT HURT US

"THERE IS NO SUCH THING AS GOOD OR BAD WHEN IT COMES TO THE BODY."

secure groundedness, we express the emotion from secure groundedness. Instead of tossing the emotion back like a hot potato, we can let it settle, unwrap its foil and savour what's inside with all its delicious toppings.

We can begin safely connecting to our emotions again through somatic work. Somatic trauma resolution practitioner and friend denise chang defines somatics as any practice that allows us to:

- go into deeper connection with our body

- have a deeper understanding of how our body communicates to us

"There is no such thing as good or bad when it comes to the body. It's all information for us to learn how to create more capacity to meet intensity and difficulty in life."

DENISE CHANG

Asana yoga, qigong and breathwork are all somatic practices, but what differentiates a somatic practice from physical exercise is the intention to notice our relationship to our physiological sensations. This means slowing down and practicing with intention. The ability to notice and understand how our body is feeling inside is called *interoception*. We can practice this awareness through a full-body scan meditation.

MEDITATION: FULL-BODY SCAN

This meditation will guide you in connecting inside your body, starting from the top of your head all the way down to the soles of your feet. You can be seated, standing or lying down.

Settle in.
Take a deep breath in.
Deep breath out.
Soften your gaze or close your eyes.

Begin by feeling the sensation of air moving in and out of your nostrils.
Focus on that sensation until you feel familiar with it.

As we take our next deep breath, let the breath travel all the way up to the top of your head. Stay there until you are familiar with the feeling.

Take a deep breath. Travel down between your temples. Unfurl your brows.
Stay here. See if you can sense the space between the front of your eyes to the back of your head.

Take a deep breath. Travel down to your jaw.
Unclench and stretch your jaw.
Stay here. See if you can sense the space in your throat and jaw.

Take a deep breath. Travel down to your shoulders and chest.
Stretch your shoulders out. Stay here. See if you can sense your heart space.

Take a deep breath. Travel down your ribcage and belly, expanding your ribcage and belly with the breath. Stay here. See if you can sense your belly space.

Take a deep breath. Travel down to the base of your spine, gently moving your hips in circles.
Stay here. See if you can sense the space between your tailbone and belly button.

Take a deep breath. Travel down your legs, ankles and feet, stretching them. Stay here. See if you can sense the inside of your legs all the way down to the bottoms of your feet.

Feeling the earth beneath you, take a deep breath in and out.
Thank yourself for this practice. Flutter your eyes open if they have been closed.

By noticing the physical sensations that come up in your body, you begin to be more open and curious when these sensations arise.

CORE EMOTIONS

Dr Hilary Jacobs Hendel's research shares that humans have seven core emotions: fear, anger, grief, joy, excitement, disgust and sexual excitement. Noticing the physical and mental relationship you have with each emotion will expand your capacity to hold it. Just as a tidal wave ebbs and flows, when the emotion passes, there is calmness and clarity.

How does each emotion feel in your body? Take your time to be curious with each emotion as it comes up. Ride the wave. See if you can express the emotion through writing, drawing and moving your body.

• Joy

....
....
....
....

• Excitement

....
....
....
....

• Fear

....
....
....
....
....
....

• Anger

....
....
....
....
....
....

• Grief

....
....
....
....
....
....

- Disgust

....
....
....
....
....
....
....
....
....

- Sexual Excitement

....
....
....
....
....
....
....
....

By befriending your emotions as an adult, you show your inner child that it is okay to do the same. You no longer need to be the child who has to fit into a neat box or sabotages yourself in order to receive attention.

The next time you hear your inner child saying, "Help! Pay attention to me! I am feeling _____," rest assured that they are coming to you for help because you are ready and they trust you. They are inviting you to take a closer look at where they are hurting. They, too, are a person with depths and complexities.

You can now tell them, "Inner Child, I see you feeling _____ Even when you are feeling _____, I am still here."

WHICH EMOTIONS HAVE YOU AND YOUR INNER CHILD NEEDED TO SUPPRESS?

REFLECTION

Which emotions have you and your inner child needed to suppress?

....
....
....
....

How would you like to honour these emotions together?

....
....
....
....

Though we may experience our emotions differently from one another, emotions connect us as human beings. Time after time, you know the feelings will pass. You will feel better equipped in trusting yourself as you ride difficult emotions. Letting yourself know, "I have ridden this wave before. Let me stay here for a while longer." In this liminal space, this pause, you find who you are and the choices you can make to align with your true self.

BEING VULNERABLE AS AN INNER PARENT

As your own inner parent, you may absorb the fears and insecurities that your own outer caretakers had. As a child, my parents were afraid of my emotions. We never had conversations that involved how we really felt. And when I expressed my emotions, I was met with either avoidance, anger, or rejection. "Don't talk back" or "Why do you cry so much?" All I wanted was to be heard and validated as a kid. But my emotions felt too much for my parents to handle because they were overwhelmed by their own.

As my own inner parent, I notice when my inner child isn't feeling well, my inner parent wants to run away.

BEING VULNERABLE

AS AN INNER PARENT

Not because they don't care for my inner child, but because my inner parent fears they cannot be there for her in a good-enough way. I remind myself that my inner child does not want me to take her pain away. My inner child wants to know I am here for her and that she will not be abandoned.

My inner parent can now tell my inner child, "I am sorry I was afraid. It is not because I am afraid of you. I was afraid that I would not be enough. I am here now. Let me be with you."

When you feel your inner child is suffering, notice what feelings, sensations and impulses come up for you as the inner parent.

When your inner child is sad, do you feel like avoiding them and running away?

When your inner child is angry, what comes up for you as an inner parent?

Your inner child is not asking you to take their discomfort away and there is no way you can truly free them from pain. Once you are at peace with that, you can genuinely show up for their experience rather than shaping it to ease your own discomfort.

A mantra your inner parent can use is, "We have been here before. I know this will pass." The longer you stay in this place of discomfort, the larger your capacity to hold your inner child becomes. You will be able to support your inner child without needing to fix or save them. Imagine how it would feel to be present with your inner child's suffering or whatever they are going through. How would that change the way you show up and react in your relationship with them?

By communicating openly with your inner child, you are teaching them that you, too, have healthy vulnerabilities as an adult.

SUPPORT YOUR INNER CHILD WITHOUT NEEDING TO FIX OR SAVE THEM

ACTIVITY

Inner Parent, write an honest letter to your inner child, with what your flaws may be, what you are still learning. Share a promise you feel is fitting.

"I am here with you. I am honoured to be a home for you."

Again, pay attention to what resonates.

....

....

....

....

....

....

....

....

....

....

....

....

....

....

....

....

....

GRIEVING THE CHILDHOOD WE LOST

When I was little, I loved pleasing my parents. My dad would call me *con gái rượu*, Daddy's girl in Vietnamese. I was the big sister who took care of my younger brother, and the eldest daughter who was good at listening to my mom's woes while keeping my father in a good mood. For the longest time, I felt like the glue holding our family together. It was too much for a young child.

Somewhere along the way, I began to hide parts of myself so I could fit the image I *thought* they wanted of me. My ten-year-old self who spilled Nesquik on the kitchen counter could clean up the cocoa drink powder so quickly, I felt like she would win if there was a game show called "Hide Your Mess!" I think of that ten-year-old now and want her to know that it's okay to make messes. It's okay to spill things. I will still love her, even when she's messy.

I became skilled at fulfilling roles and duties, so that when I met people later in life who didn't expect the same of me, I felt like I had nothing to give. I was surprised they didn't need me to do anything. They only wanted to be in my presence.

I think back to my two-year-old self, who was not ready to be a big sister and take care of my younger sibling. Like any other child, I willingly took on the role of mini caretaker because it made my parents happy and earned me the praise I craved. I love my younger sibling and because of that, it made it harder for me to acknowledge that taking on the role of a big sister so early on in my life was difficult for me. I thought that acknowledging the unhappiness I felt would diminish the love I feel for my sibling, but it doesn't. In fact, it makes it easier for me to love my sibling more because I know loving them won't mean sacrificing myself. I get to share with them what I need, my own boundaries, and how I would like to be supported by them.

With the help of my therapist, I was finally able to see the part of me that felt unseen. My inner child wanted to be Mommy and Daddy's little girl forever. She had yearned to bask in her parents' love for a little longer – to not be responsible for so many things that felt out of her control and out of her abilities. She longed to be a child.

One day while shopping at a local stationery store, a sticker sheet caught my eye. It had illustrations of a little girl with short black hair, cropped like the cap of a mushroom. The best part of all, she was alongside her mom and dad. There were stickers of them playing, bickering with each other, cuddling together.

I smiled gleamingly. This was the reality my inner child had been searching for, a reality where she was the centre of her mummy's and daddy's universe. In that moment I felt sadness, grief and joy.

Though we can't change the past, we can hold grief and sadness with our inner child. We can grieve for the childhood we wanted but didn't have.

Grief is often associated with the death of a loved one or physical death, but every day we have moments where we grieve what could have been. To grieve our past selves is to let our inner child know their experience matters.

REFLECTION

Inner Child, how can I sit with you in your sadness and grief?

What is one small way we can honour your grief?

Answer from my inner child:

....
....
....
....
....
....
....
....
....
....

"tiffany, I would like you to slow down with me, to hold me, to take a bath and cry with me. I would like you to not push my friends away, instead share how I feel with them. I would like to know my grief is not too big for you to hold."

WHAT IS ONE SMALL WAY WE CAN HONOUR YOUR GRIEF?

HONESTY HURTS, AND YET TRUE HEALING COMES FROM HONESTY

HONOURING YOUR GRIEF

When we begin to acknowledge our grief, it may feel as though we are betraying our caretakers: family, or whoever it was, who couldn't give us what we needed. Part of being an adult and taking care of our inner child means recognizing and accepting that our parents can't do everything for us. Even when our needs aren't met, they are still valid. Honouring your grief doesn't hurt anyone, but it sure can be painful.

Honesty hurts, and yet true healing comes from honesty.

I grieve for my younger self who wanted parents who grew up in the same country and spoke the same language easily, so that they could understand my struggles. I grieve for my younger self who wanted to express her emotions freely but was told not to cry. I grieve for my grade-school self who wanted to have a solid group of best friends, but had to say goodbye to them when I moved or they moved. I grieve for my high-school self who wanted to explore her individuality but was met with fear when she did. I grieve for my queer self, who didn't get to be expressed or discovered until adulthood. I grieve for all the parts of me who needed to hide, so that they could feel safe as a child. To grieve is to make space for our own truth and experience.

REFLECTION

Which parts of yourself would you like to grieve?

....

....

....

....

Which parts did you need to abandon to feel safe?

....

....

....

....

How would you like to reclaim those parts now?

....

....

....

....

How does your inner child feel about that?

....

....

....

....

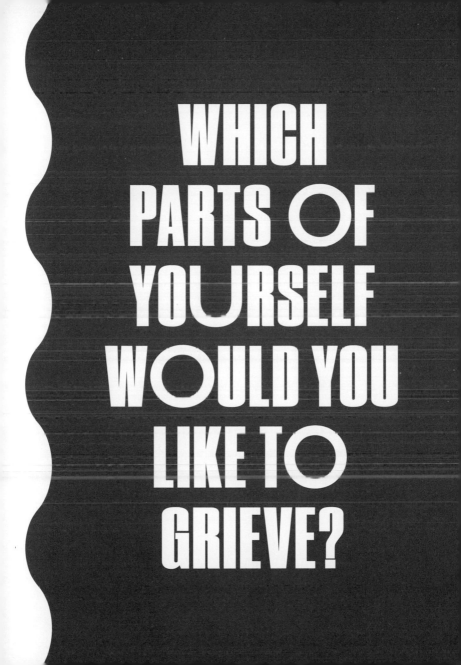

WHICH PARTS OF YOURSELF WOULD YOU LIKE TO GRIEVE?

SELF-PUNISHMENT AND SELF-FORGIVENESS

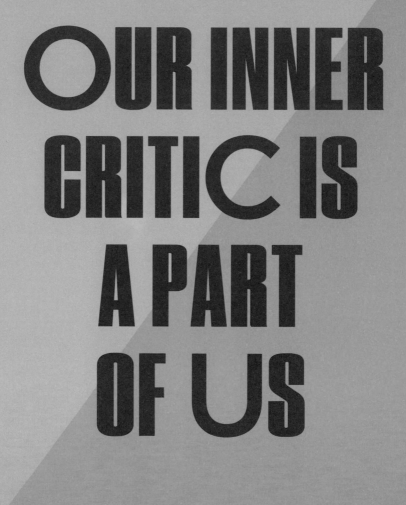

OUR INNER CRITIC IS A PART OF US

"You're not good enough."

We've all heard this voice inside ourselves. Perhaps we've become good friends with this voice. It's been there for us through the hard times, through deadlines we thought we couldn't finish, through major accomplishments. Perhaps we're scared that if we let go of this inner critic, our life will fall apart. We'll have no more self-discipline, and how could we possibly get anything done?

It's easy to collect reasons to keep our inner critic around. At the same time, we want to push them away, but our inner critic is like anyone else. They get tired, too. Ironically enough, our inner critic is actually critical of themselves, afraid that if they stop punishing you, they won't be doing their job. They won't be protecting you well. So, what would happen if we invited them inside our inner home? What would we learn?

Once we sit with our inner critic, we begin to understand our voice of self-punishment comes from a time when we were vulnerable and trying to protect ourselves. In a way, our inner critic is a part of us, our inner child frozen in time, believing that we need to do x, y, z to remain safe from harm or from being an outcast.

So far in the book, we have been working with the inner child and inner parent, but we have many more inner voices. The Internal Family Systems model (IFS) developed by Dr Richard Schwartz gives our inner parts specific names, beyond the "inner parent" and "inner child". IFS focuses on how each of our parts have their own full-fledged stories of why they act the way they do and are caught up in the extreme role they had to take on during a certain incident, period of time or situation. IFS notes that when we are aware of the trauma these parts carry, we can spreak to them directly and release them of their "burdens", like letting your inner critic know they can retire from being a security guard. Once these parts let go of that burden, they can become a supportive, loving part of ourselves. This is similar to how our inner parent can be overly critical, but once allowed to let go of their overly protective role, they become our own nurturing inner caretakers.

There are many days when speaking to myself with compassion feels like an out-of-reach ideal, but day by day, I find small moments to renegotiate with myself. When I see my pile of dirty laundry, I can hear my inner critic say, "You're so lazy. What would people think if they saw this?" And I have the chance to respond kindly back, "We have had a long week, haven't we? So much has happened. What if we asked a friend to keep us company to do laundry this week? Wouldn't that be fun?"

LET YOUR INNER CRITIC KNOW THEY CAN RETIRE

Changing how we speak to ourselves most definitely will be met with resistance. As we practice being kinder to ourselves, we become better at noticing when others are speaking critically towards themselves or to us. These moments become a chance for us to invite them and ourselves back into the practice of self-compassion.

INVITE YOURSELF BACK INTO THE PRACTICE OF SELF-COMPASSION

REFLECTION

What is your inner critic telling you today?

....

....

....

....

....

Invite them to share the duties they are feeling towards you.

How can you help them release these duties?

....

....

....

....

....

As you embrace your inner critic, you:

- **release old patterns of self-destructiveness**
  Understanding that you can trust yourself and you
  also deserve good things.

- **attune with your natural rhythms and seasons**
  You can slow down and tune into your body's
  unique timing, rather than following a beat that
  doesn't align with you, such as toxic productivity.

- **respect your own worthiness and the worthiness
  of others**
  By respecting your true self, not the side that's
  self-driven by fear and punishment, you protect
  yourself from being exploited by others, as well as
  from unconsciously exploiting others.

I would like to acknowledge that the practice of
holding your inner critic in community and with
trusted people in your life is just as important
as doing so on your own. The wounds you have
developed as a child through interpersonal
connections can also be healed through
interpersonal connection. Through vulnerability
and asking for the support you need, you are
shown the ultimate truth. You are lovable even in
your imperfection.

YOU ARE LOVABLE EVEN IN YOUR IMPERFECTION

SELF-FORGIVENESS

Self-forgiveness is a radical act of love and commitment to yourself, turning away from the guilt you've carried with you since childhood. Through forgiveness, you accept yourself as a growing, healing being. Forgiving yourself does not mean you are enabling harmful habits or patterns. Rather, it means you acknowledge the mistakes and the pain you may have caused while freeing yourself of the past, so you can be present and make choices from a place of clarity.

ALLOW SPACE FOR

PEACE AND COMFORT

When healing your inner child, you can forgive yourself for not knowing how to support your inner child earlier.

By forgiving myself, I release myself from the cycle of self-punishment and blame.

By forgiving myself, I meet the root of my hurt and pain with loving tenderness.

Forgiveness can be practiced in big and small ways. Setting time aside at the end of the day to forgive yourself and release the expectations you didn't fulfil will help you start the next day anew.

TRUSTING YOUR FLOW

"It may feel like nothing is happening on the surface, but that is because we are starting the change from our roots."

DOHEE LEE, ARTIST, RITUALIST,
AND FOUNDER OF PURI ARTS

There will be many times when you feel like nothing is changing or that you are regressing. Trust your process. Connecting with your inner child will bring up past traumas and tender moments alike. This work isn't to be rushed.

When you find yourself wanting to sign up for every workshop and to read every book, let yourself feel that excitement and relish in it. Then pause and make room to contemplate what about it draws you in. How are you already practicing this in your life? More importantly, do you have the capacity for this? If not, how can you integrate or explore this in a way that honours where you are in your journey? Whether the answer is yes, no or maybe, you'll be clear on your why.

The times you spend resting will be just as important as the times you're uprooting.

Cam, a past coaching client of mine eloquently wrote, "If I were a vast field, the past few weeks have been a gradual process of clearing and overturning the land inside me that was once filled with weeds, the dying remains of last season's harvest, and clots of soil that were stubborn and resistant to breaking down into something softer. [I am] realizing that there are many parts of me that need gentle care and attention before myself and my dreams can blossom."

At times your healing will feel fast and at other times you will feel so slow. Noticing which season your inner garden is in and how you need to tend to it is part of this work.

SPEAKING IN YOUR MOTHER TONGUE

Speaking Vietnamese was never my strong suit. Though it was the first language I was raised with, once I began school English took priority. When I did speak Vietnamese, I felt half my age. I didn't know how to read or write it and most of what I learned came from listening to my parents speak or greeting my elders in broken blessings.

It wasn't until my late twenties, when I began practicing the language with my friends that I felt my Vietnamese catching up with my English self. As I became more confident in my relationship with the language, the desire to express myself in Vietnamese

THE RESONANCE OF WORDS IS AS IMPORTANT AS THEIR MEANING

emerged. Alongside the plates of cut fruit and the back rubs my mom gave me to fall asleep, my fondest memories always went back to being called Nì. This was an endearing nickname given by my parents pronounced Nee, like Tif-fun-nee. These memories offer me inspiration, ways to take care of my inner child that felt special to me.

I began to journal or speak to my inner child in Vietnamese, welcoming her with the same name: "*Nì ơi, Nì à.*" Singsongly, just as my mom would call for me when I was young. Though my inner critic resisted and cringed, I told myself it was okay to write Vietnamese without the proper accents and even to misspell words if it helped me get the thoughts and feelings across to my own inner child – and it was true! My inner child didn't care about the misspellings. She loved the fact that she was being spoken to in a language she felt familiar with.

The resonance of words is as important as their meaning. When I say, "*Mẹ thương con* (I love you)" there is a tenderness that can't be conveyed through its English translation.

If you grew up speaking more than one language, I welcome you to notice how you feel with each language.

REFLECTION

Does one language bring out parts of you that another doesn't?

Do you have a language you feel particularly comforted by?

If so, what are the phrases of love, endearment and encouragement that resonate with you? Try the phrases out for yourself. Say them aloud.

Speaking in your mother tongue may not necessarily mean speaking in a different language. You can still look back to when you were younger and reflect on the ways you were shown love, endearment or encouragement. Did these ways resonate with you? Which acts of care would you like to adopt for yourself?

What does the term "mother tongue" mean to you?

WHAT DOES THE TERM "MOTHER TONGUE" MEAN TO YOU?

A VILLAGE
OF SUPPORT

I won't pretend this work is easy. It is brave to hold ourselves. To go deep, to explore our inner depths. There are moments when I am afraid of my inner child's pain. When it feels too much, too heart-wrenching to hold. When I want to run away, hide in a hole, hoping the pain will magically go away. Then there are times when I run towards it, dive headfirst, grasping my pain tightly, asking, "Why are you still here? Why aren't you healed yet?" But in the moments where I am brave to be soft, brave to be where I am, I see that the thing I'm so afraid of – myself – isn't scary at all.

Like everyone else, you will have moments when you think, "I can't do this. I just can't." And that's okay. You weren't meant to do it alone.

It takes a village to raise a child. Living in a hyper individualistic society robs us of this reality. I remember wishing for friends, for community, for family who cared about me in the ways I needed. I felt alone in my experience, searching for a way to bridge my reality as a child of refugees and as an American. When I found friends, I wasn't sure how to ask for help. When I had community, I thought, "I don't really belong here anyways." When I was around family, all I could think of were the responsibilities and obligations that it came with. I thought my solution to not feeling enough was to love myself harder, tighten the reins and double down on the idea that "I can only be loved when I love myself fully." One of toxic independence. It took meeting people who were generous with their love to show me how to receive in ways I thought impossible. Chosen family, friends and kind souls showed me I didn't need to love myself alone. Being open to receive the love and support I so dearly wanted took time and practice. As I practiced speaking to myself and my inner child compassionately, my capacity to love and receive love grew, too.

Only through community and the collective spirit can you support your inner child in all the stages and in different aspects of their growth.

FRIENDS

In a world that epitomizes romantic relationships, friendships are equally as important. Friendships are free from the history of arranged marriages and familial obligations. Friendship is a powerful and accessible way for us to practice nurturing safe, secure relationships with one another.

Ways I have included my friends in my journey are:

- normalizing the multitude of my inner voices in my everyday conversations with friends. "My inner child is feeling _____."

- asking friends to go on inner child play dates with me.

My voice of resistance when asking friends for help says, "They don't really want to be your friend. They're busy. You don't want to come off as clingy." Time and time again, when I reach out to my friends, I am shown they want to be there for me, especially when I make it safe for them to speak their needs genuinely.

An example of how to ask for help consensually:

- **Me:** I would like your support in _____. Do you have the capacity?

- **Friend:** I'm not available in that way, but I can offer _____.

In this way, you can practice being in relationships that are mutually supportive and freeing. You and your friend can be in genuine existence.

PRACTICE BEING IN RELATIONSHIPS THAT ARE MUTUALLY SUPPORTIVE AND FREEING

REFLECTION

What affirmation would you like to tell yourself when you are uncertain of whether or not to reach out to a friend?

....
....
....
....
....
....
....
....
....
....
....
....
....

Hint, close your eyes and imagine what that friend would say to you!

ANCESTORS

Being born from a diaspora, my ancestors are what connect me to Vietnam, a country I could have called home. My ancestors are the resilience and strength of my people. They hold generations of knowledge within them.

When my *Bà Ngoại*, my maternal grandma, was diagnosed with terminal acute leukaemia, I knew her passing would be symbolic. She was the woman who took care of me as a child, my last living maternal ancestor. Before she passed, I didn't resonate with the cultural rituals my family performed to honour our ancestors, but after her passing I found comfort in lighting incense at her altar and offering her food as a way to connect. I feel her presence within me every day, asking her for words of wisdom when in need of reassurance. Through her, I know I am supported by those who came before me.

REFLECTION

Are there ancestors, living or deceased, you look towards?

....
....
....
....
....
....
....
....
....
....
....
....

Explore rituals and ways to help you connect with their spirit and guidance.

ARE THERE ANCESTORS, LIVING OR DECEASED, YOU LOOK TOWARDS?

I AVOIDED CLOSE RELATIONSHIPS WITH FAMILY

FAMILY

Listening to my parents' arguments as a child, I came to believe that their disagreements were the fault of my extended family. I came to the conclusion that having any relationship with extended family equalled drama and chaos. As my inner parent tried to protect my inner child from her past, I avoided close relationships with family and told myself I didn't want or need them in my life. Yet as I begin to heal, I begin to see each family member for who they are - people who are healing, too.

When I visited Texas to see off my *Bà Ngoại*, I found great surprise in reconnecting with my uncle, *Câu Hien*. We never talked much before, but this time felt different. Amid the whirlwind of funeral preparations for my grandma, he became a source of levity and love for me. Though he had just lost his mom to cancer, he was the one person in my family who checked in to ask me how I was doing. He shared his boat stories with me, from when he fled Vietnam after the Fall of Saigon - stories my family didn't dare to retell, let alone share in vivid detail. He spoke to me in both Vietnamese and English in an attempt to meet me halfway. With my family, a part of me had always felt erased and misunderstood, but here was an elder who wanted to understand both sides of me, my American self and my Vietnamese self. As I used English to fill in my gaps of expression, seamlessly, he used Vietnamese to fill in his. Through our bilingual conversations, both his inner child and my inner child felt seen in their struggle of living, wedged between two cultures.

REFLECTION

Have you been surprised by any moments with family members?

....
....
....
....
....
....
....
....
....
....
....
....
....
....
....
....

TEACHERS AND GUIDES

As someone who finds great joy in learning, I have found solace in staying in touch with many of my past teachers. I'd like to specifically thank my former design professor, James Housefield, whom I am happy to call my friend and to be in creative mentorship with one another.

Whenever I'm unsure of my own creative voice, I ask myself, "What would James say?" James has shown me that my voice is important in more ways than I can imagine. His humility and curiosity as a teacher has reminded me over and over again that no matter my age, gender or title, no voice of authority is greater than my own.

VISUALIZATION

Who has been a teacher or guide in your life?

How would you like to integrate their voice into your life?

Invite yourself to visualize yourself in front of them.

What would they like to tell you in times of self-doubt and self-trust?

COMMUNITY IS FINDING SAFETY IN THE COLLECTIVE

COMMUNITY

Community is a place for me to see my inner self reflected external. Community is evidence that I belong – through shared experiences, interests, intentions and identities. Community is finding safety in the collective.

From joining the Vietnamese Student Association in college on a whim to creating a writing club with my friends, some communities you find by chance, some through intention. When I first join a community   , my voice of resistance tells me, "You don't belong here. People already have their own group going on." To soothe this voice, I imagine how it would feel for me to belong in this community. What if I gave myself a chance to belong? Braver yet, what if I gave myself a chance to contribute to this community? What would that look like?

As a homebody myself, it can be hard to get out of the house. It helped me immensely to either focus on connecting with one person at a time in the community or signing up to be a volunteer. By volunteering, I came in with an existing sense of camaraderie. Gathering by gathering, I accepted more of myself and the possibility that perhaps not only do I belong, my presence makes a difference.

REFLECTION

What kind of communal support are you looking for right now?

....
....
....
....
....
....
....

BEING OPEN TO

COMMUNAL SUPPORT

How can you stay open to that support?

....
....
....
....
....
....
....
....
....

PROFESSIONAL SUPPORT

In addition to the support I mention above, there are focused resources we can look for, such as support through one-on-one therapy, group therapy, local community programmes, peer support groups and coaching. Receiving support from trained professionals can give us a new perspective, free from the biases of those in our personal lives. I have been privileged to work with a wide range of coaches and therapists because of the field I work in, yet I am aware that mental health resources aren't as accessible to everyone.

In my search, I have been inspired and amazed by the work that my local community organizations, non-profits and practitioners have put out there, some of whom offer services at a low or sliding scale cost. You can search up organizations in your local community with keywords that match your personal identities, areas of interest and how you'd like to be supported. Once you reach out to one organization or practitioner, they likely will have a network of resources they can connect you with. There are also organizations, such as Open Path Collective, that exist to connect clients to affordable, accessible mental healthcare.

There are a few things I wish I knew while seeking therapy, coaching, or any other professional support. The first is you are the number one person who knows what you need. When you begin asking for help, even when you feel uncertain in expressing your need, trust yourself. The process of learning to express is healing in itself, especially if we were discouraged or punished for expressing our true needs as a child. In these moments you can ask the other person for help in expressing what you need. You can say, "A need is coming up, and I would like help identifying it." Along the same vein, if you feel your wellness practitioner is not supporting you in the ways you would like, let them know. A therapist, coach or supporter who is the right match for you will be receptive and grateful you are helping them help you.

Secondly, as someone recovering from being a "good student" and collecting stamps of approval, I would tell myself:

1   Go to therapy for yourself, not to check off another box.

2   You don't need to be in therapy to be healing.

At the end of the day, you don't go to therapy because you are broken. You go to therapy because you deserve a space that honours your whole self.

Here are some questions you can ask when looking for a therapist, kindly provided by Dr Trish Phillips, who specializes in inner child healing. You can ask them:

- Can you share with me what therapy is like?

- How may a session with you look? How often do you recommend me to see you and can there be flexibility in frequency to accommodate my needs?

- Do you have experience with Inner Child work on whatever my present concern is?

- Are you familiar with Internal Family Systems or Parts Work? Do you work with attachment styles?

- Can I reach out to you when I am feeling dysregulated between our sessions?

You can always ask a therapist if they offer sliding scale payments or for more referrals and resources to help you find the right match. Finding the right person to support you in your journey may take some time and a few tries. Don't give up, even if the process is difficult, because the support you're looking for wants to find you too.

Western psychology has historically focused on individualism, placing heavy responsibility on the individual to heal oneself. However, if we are to see ourselves as existing within a community, a village, an ecosystem, connected and interdependent, how does that change our view of healing? How may we begin to support each other in healing?

HEALING SEVEN GENERATIONS FORWARD AND BACKWARDS

Look at me. I am human.
See me. I am not erased.
Hear me. I am not silenced.
Feel me. For I am free.

Writing this book, I have felt the duality of grief and celebration. My heart has broken and come together over and over again. Once this book is published, I will have done what I have been afraid to do. To honour my inner child with tenderness and care. To say yes, her perspective matters.

I have been told what generations before me have been told not to do: "Don't air your dirty laundry. What will the neighbours think?" To that I say, "Sure, my laundry is dirty, but all clothes need love, care and washing at some point. And maybe ... just maybe, we can even wash them together."

I share my story to release the burden of silence. The burden that generations before me have carried. As the eldest daughter of an eldest daughter, my mom, I grew up seeing her slave away, holding her self-worth so tightly to how much of herself she could give up. No more, I say. Let me break the toxic cycle that has kept our inner child captive. I relieve myself of the illusion that everything, everyone, depends on me. I release the idea that I am a sacrificial body – so selfless that I am no longer human.

Inspired by an Iroquois philosophy, my friend and storytelling coach Haylee Thikeo writes, "When you heal yourself, you are healing seven generations before you, and seven generations after you."

Through honouring my own inner child, I honour my mother's, my father's and my grandparents' inner children, too. Even when we don't have the words to speak about our inner children together, I feel their healing. I see it in the way that their joy and wonder come more quickly, more easily, when I give them a playful birthday gift or when my parents pause to tell me they do – in fact – love me. There are the moments I thought I would never get to have, ones I didn't dare dream of.

Your story may look different from mine,
but I know one thing that's for sure.
Your inner child is here and waiting for you,
and they definitely want to say,
"I love you."

YOUR INNER CHILD IS HERE AND WAITING FOR YOU, AND THEY DEFINITELY WANT TO SAY, "I LOVE YOU."

Cảm ơn, con thương Mẹ and Ba. I love you. I know it's scary, but let's grow together.

Thank you to my sibling, Kevin. You have been with me through thick and thin. I love you so much.

Thank you, Khoa, for accidentally sending me the self-parenting book and for being my life companion. Thank you, Tansy, for being my spiritual partner. Thank you, Carl, for being my dear friend and writing partner. Thank you Chica, my chihuahua, for being my late night support system. Thank you to all the friends who believed in me and edited with me: Monica, Chloe, Hirsch, Hikari, Tina, Izzy, Steven, Ngoc, Christina, Vĩ Sơn, Elina, Vivian, Serina, Canary and the rest, you know who you are.

Thank you to Our Village – a shoutout to Alyza and Paulina – the Writing Club, and all the friends I've made through the healing community: Cass, Karen, Andrea, Serena, denise, Tiffany Wong, Haylee, Jayda, Phương–Thảo, Tiff, Aly, Stephanie Lee. You help me dream of a better world. Thank you to all the Asian femmes who write, including Jamie Li, Jessica Nguyen, Giovanna Lomanto and Susan Lieu. Thank you to my communities, online and offline. Your support doesn't go unnoticed! You have seen me through my many transformations.

Thank you to James Housefield for being the human you are. To Soonja Kim for your very important remothering work. To Dr Trish Phillips, aka The Doodle Doc, for your sincere commitment to inner child healing. To Dohee Lee for your vulnerability and intuition as a leader.

And of course, thank you to Millie, my editor, for lending me your words in the Self-Forgiveness chapter and for trusting me with this book.

RESOURCES

Attachment theory
Attachment theory, researched by Mary Ainsworth and John Bowlby, suggests how we relate to others as adults is based on how receptive our caregivers were to our needs as children. The good news is that knowing about the different attachment styles can help us to see our own relational patterns and give us information on how to shift our behaviour in ways that support us in feeling more secure in our relationships. The four attachment styles defined are: secure, anxious-avoidant, anxious-ambivalent and anxious-disorganized.

Complex trauma
Complex trauma describes traumas compounded over time rather than a single, traumatic event. This can look like living in household dysfunction or experiencing neglect over time. It may feel difficult to validate ourselves when we don't have a single, traumatic event to point back to, but the chronic traumas that our inner child has experienced deserve an equal amount of attention. I wanted to include this definition to remind us that no traumas are too small to tend to if these are important to us and our inner child.

Parenting styles
Learning about parenting styles gives us context to how we were parented as children, as well as providing

us with a model of how we can parent our own inner child. In 1966, Dr Diana Baumrind pioneered the four styles of authoritarian, authoritative, permissive and neglectful.

Polyvagal theory
Polyvagal theory, developed by Dr Stephen W. Porges, illustrates how our physiological state affects our psychological state. This is a fancy way of saying that our body is connected to our mind. Many of us are familiar with the nervous system's fight, flight, freeze response. The polyvagal theory highlights our ventral vagus nerve, a nerve that runs down the course of our spine connecting our brain and our body together. This nerve is central to us returning to a feeling of balance and safety. Learning about the polyvagal theory can help you identify the states of dysregulation and how to regulate your body back to inner safety.

Reactions to shame: flight, fight, fawn, freeze
Of the four sympathetic nervous system's responses, we know flight, fight, and freeze the best. Fawning is the fourth, lesser known response. The Reactions to Shame chart, developed by Bret Lyon and Sheila Rubin, defines fawning as working to please the source of a threat, even when it is a detriment to yourself, in hopes of staying safe or in relationship with the other party. With this knowledge, you can develop healthier ways to react to situations, ways that value both your own well-being and the other party's.

tiffany trieu (thanh nguyệt) is a Vietnamese American writer, artist, inner child advocate and community organizer. Her practice has grown from her own personal journey, being a child of the Vietnamese Diaspora and a queer person. This is her first book.

READING LIST

The Drama of the Gifted Child: The Search for the True Self, Alice Miller

The Good Neighbor: The Life and Work of Fred Rogers, Maxwell King

No Bad Parts: Healing Trauma and Restoring Wholeness with The Internal Family Systems Model, Richard Schwartz, PhD

The Power of Discord: Why the Ups and Downs of Relationships Are the Secret to Building Intimacy, Resilience, and Trust, Claudia M. Gold, MD and Ed Tronick, PhD

Self-Parenting: The Complete Guide to Your Inner Conversations, Dr. John K Pollard III

Teaching As A Subversive Activity, Neil Postman and Charles Weingartner

Windows to Our Children: A Gestalt Therapy Approach to Children and Adolescents, Violet Oaklander